Tarantulas

By Christy Steele

STECK-VAUGHN
ELEMENTARY · SECONDARY · ADULT · LIBRARY

A Harcourt Company

www.steck-vaughn.com

ANIMALS OF THE RAIN FOREST

Library of Congress Cataloging-in-Publication Data is available upon request.

Printed and bound in the United States of America
10 9 8 7 6 5 4 3 2 1 W 04 03 02 01

Photo Acknowledgments
Corbis/Dewitt Jones, 26
James C. Cokendolpher, 25
Rick West, title page, 4-5, 6, 10, 13, 14, 18, 20, 22, 28
Visuals Unlimited/G and C Merker, cover; ESA-Riess, 16

Contents

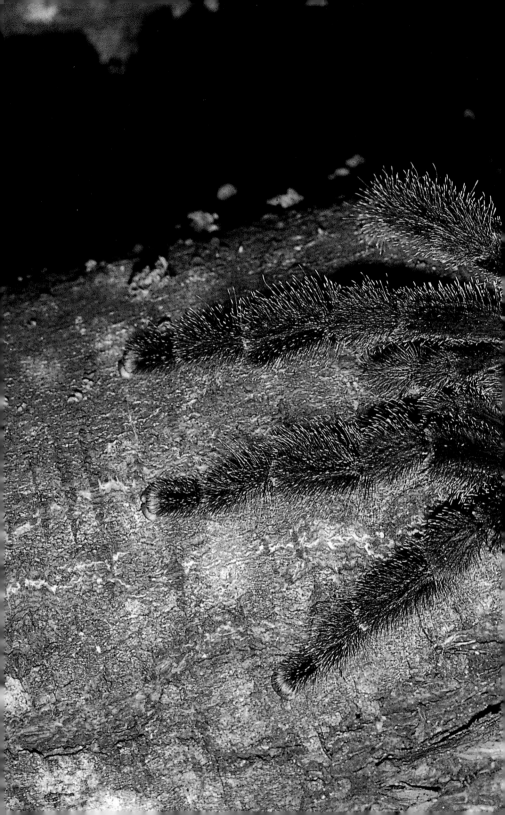

MEXICO

BELIZE
HONDURAS
GUATEMALA   NICARAGUA
EL SALVADOR   *Caribbean Sea*

COSTA RICA   VENEZUELA
PANAMA
COLOMBIA
ECUADOR

North Atlantic Ocean

GUYANA
SURINAME
FRENCH GUIANA (FRANCE)

AMAZON RIVER

PERU   BRAZIL

BOLIVIA

South Pacific Ocean

PARAGUAY
CHILE

South Atlantic Ocean

ARGENTINA   URUGUAY

Rain-Forest Range of the Tarantula in Central and South America

Surrounding Land

Water

Borders

Rivers

N
W   E
S

A Quick Look at Tarantulas

What do tarantulas look like?

Tarantulas are hairy spiders. Some of them are very large. They can be many different colors.

How many kinds of tarantulas are there?

There are 800 known kinds of tarantulas.

Where do tarantulas live?

Tarantulas live in warm places around the world. They do not live in Antarctica.

What do tarantulas eat?

Tarantulas eat meat. They catch and eat insects, frogs, lizards, mice, and other small animals. They also eat spiders and other tarantulas.

Arañas peludas is the Latin American nickname for tarantulas. It means hairy spiders.

About Tarantulas

Tarantulas are hairy spiders. There are about 800 known kinds of tarantulas. Scientists think there are even more kinds of tarantulas they have not found yet. Some tarantulas are the largest spiders in the world.

Tarantulas live in most warm parts of the world. They do not live in Antarctica. It is too cold in Antarctica for tarantulas. Many kinds of tarantulas live in rain forests. Rain forests are places where many trees and plants grow close together and rain falls most of the time. Tarantulas are important to the rain forest. They eat many insects.

This tarantula's coloring helps it blend in with tree bark.

A tarantula has its own territory where it lives and hunts. Territories are close to their burrows or nests. A burrow is a hole where an animal lives. Tarantulas fight other tarantulas that come into their territories.

Tarantula Size and Coloring

Tarantulas can be many different sizes. Males are usually thinner than females.

Most kinds of tarantulas have a leg span of about 5 inches (13 cm). Their bodies are from about 1.5 inches (3.8 cm) to 4 inches (10 cm) long.

Each kind of tarantula looks different. Tarantulas' hair can be black, brown, blue, red, pink, orange, and many other colors. Some tarantulas have colorful markings or stripes on their bodies or legs.

A tarantula's hairs are its sensors. A sensor is something that can feel changes around it. Some of their hairs sense heat, cold, and motion. Hairs by a tarantula's mouth help it smell and taste.

Cephalothorax

A tarantula's body has two main parts. The front part is the **cephalothorax**. A spider's mouth, eyes, and eight legs are on this part. Two claws are on each of a tarantula's legs.

Two **chelicerae** are around a tarantula's mouth. They act like a pair of jaws. A **fang** grows on the end of each of the chelicerae. A fang is a long, pointed tooth.

A tarantula has two pedipalps. Pedipalps are about half the size of its legs. A tarantula uses its pedipalps to feel its way when walking. It also moves and grabs things like food with its pedipalps.

Abdomen

The back of a spider's body is its **abdomen**. Four spinnerets stick out from the back of the abdomen. Spiders use spinnerets to spin silk. Liquid silk is made inside tarantula's bodies. The spinnerets shape the silk into threads. The silk hardens once it is outside the body.

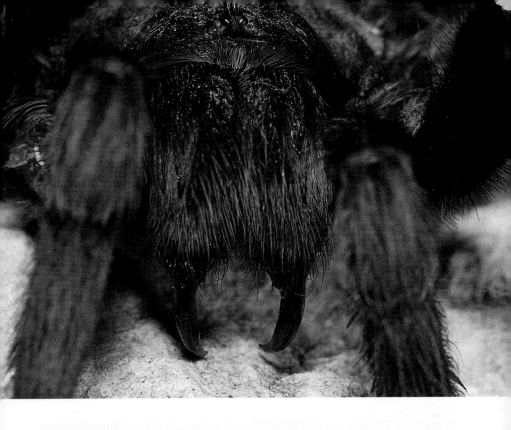

▲ A tarantula's fangs can grow up to
one-half inch (about 1 cm) long.

Some tarantulas have special hairs on the
backs of their abdomens. The hairs have very
tiny hooks on them. Tarantulas can flick the
hairs at their enemies. The hairs fly through
the air and hurt their enemies' eyes, noses,
and throats.

Silk
Nest

▲ This tree-living tarantula has spun a
tube-shaped silk nest on a tree trunk.

Ground-Living Tarantulas

There are two groups of rain-forest
tarantulas. One group stays on the ground.
Most scientists believe these tarantulas have
poor eyesight. They use their hairs to find
and catch food.

Ground-living tarantulas live in fallen logs, cracks in rocks, or **burrows**. A burrow is an underground hole or tunnel where an animal lives. Tarantulas sometimes live in burrows that other animals have left. They may also use their chelicerae to dig their own burrows. Some tarantulas spin silk to line their burrows. Others block their burrow's opening by piling dirt in front.

The second group of tarantulas lives mostly in trees. Tree-climbing tarantulas live in holes in trees or under branches and leaves. They may spin a tube-shaped nest of silk.

Tree-climbing tarantulas have **adapted** to live in trees. To be adapted means that a living thing has features that help it fit where it lives. These tarantulas often have longer legs and thinner abdomens than others. They have hundreds of stiff hairs on the bottoms of their feet. The claws and hairs help them climb. They can see better than ground-living tarantulas. This helps them jump among branches. Many of them also swim well.

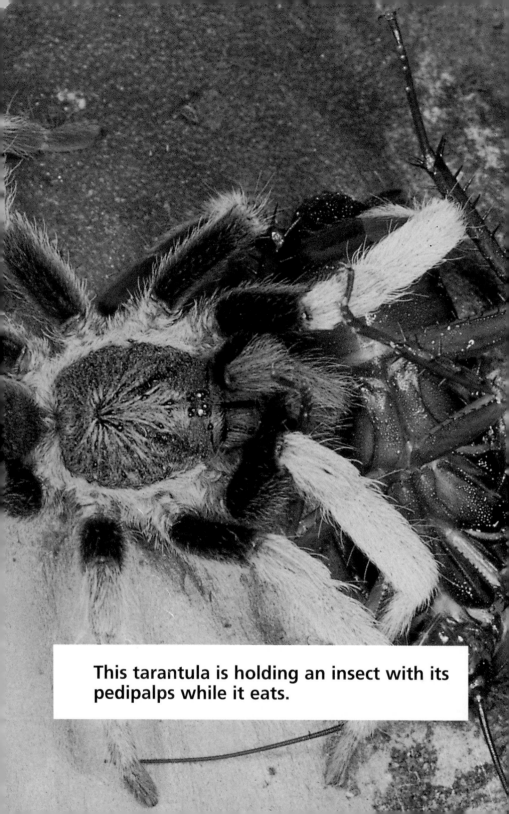

This tarantula is holding an insect with its pedipalps while it eats.

Hunting and Eating

Tarantulas are predators. A predator is an animal that hunts and eats other animals. Animals that are hunted are called prey. Tarantulas are also scavengers. A scavenger is an animal that eats food that it did not kill.

Tarantulas will eat almost anything they can catch. Insects are a common food. They often eat ants, beetles, and cockroaches. They may also eat small lizards, snakes, and frogs. They will even eat other tarantulas.

Tarantulas are **nocturnal**. Nocturnal means active during the night. They rest in their burrows during the day. At night, they come out to hunt. They never go far from their burrows when they hunt.

Tree frogs and lizards are common foods for tree-living tarantulas.

Finding and Catching Prey

Both ground-living and tree-living tarantulas find prey in the same way. A tarantula's hairs sense when prey comes near. They also use silk threads strung around their burrows or nests. The threads move when prey comes close.

Tarantulas hunt by sitting still and waiting. Some tarantulas hide in their nests or burrows. Others have colors that blend with their surroundings. This makes it hard for prey to see them. They may sit on tree branches or under leaves. Tarantulas wait until prey comes close. Then they race out and jump on prey. Tarantulas use their legs and pedipalps to hold prey still.

Tarantulas sink their sharp fangs into the prey's body. A tarantula fang is hollow with a hole in the end. When it bites, **venom** fills a tarantula's fang. Venom is a kind of poison. The tarantula pushes the venom into its prey's body. The venom makes the animal unable to move.

Tarantula mouths are so small that only liquid can fit through them. To eat, they put special digestive juices onto their prey. Digestive juices break down the prey's bodies into liquid. They cut up the prey with their chelicerae and pedipalps to help make it liquid. The tarantula drinks the liquid prey.

Only tarantulas of the same species can mate with each other.

A Tarantula's Life Cycle

Tarantulas live and hunt by themselves. They come together only to mate.

Tarantulas cannot mate until they are fully grown. This amount of time is different for each kind of tarantula. Some kinds are fully grown at two years, but others take 10 years or more to fully grow.

Male tarantulas will travel a long way to look for females. A male is careful when he finds a female. He uses his legs to tap the female's burrow. When she comes out, he taps her as well. He also may shake his legs. The tapping and shaking show her that he is not an enemy. After mating, the male leaves. Otherwise, the female may try to eat him.

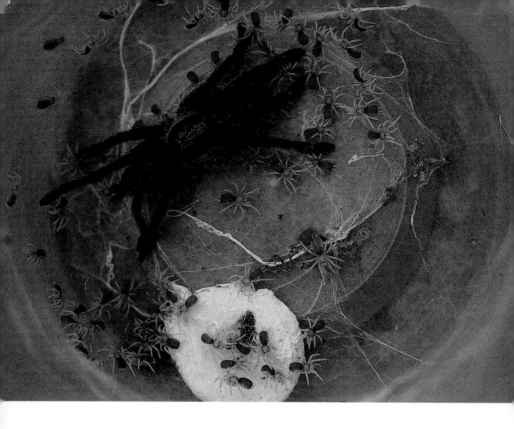

▲ Spiderlings grow inside the eggsac.
Large spiderlings eat smaller ones.

Laying Eggs

Females lay eggs several weeks or months after mating. They spin a pad of silk. They lay hundreds of eggs on the silk pad. Then they cover the eggs with more silk and seal the silk covering. This makes one large eggsac. The silk covers and keeps the eggs safe. The

Tarantula hawk wasps are enemies of tarantulas. If they meet, a tarantula hawk wasp and a tarantula will fight to the death. If the wasp wins, it stings the spider many times. The stings make the tarantula unable to move. Then, the wasp lays an egg on the tarantula's abdomen or head. When the egg hatches, the young wasp feeds on the living tarantula.

females never leave their eggsacs. They carry their eggsacs wherever they go.

Young tarantulas grow inside the eggs from one to three months. Then they hatch. After hatching, they are called **spiderlings**. Spiderlings grow inside the eggsac for awhile. Then they break out of the eggsac. Spiderlings may stay near their mother for a short time. Then they walk away to find their own burrow.

Only a few spiderlings live to become adults. Tarantulas have many enemies. Frogs, lizards, birds, insects, and other spiders eat many spiderlings. Owls, millipedes, snakes, and other animals eat adult tarantulas.

Molting

A hard, outer skin covers tarantulas. After time, new skin grows underneath the old skin. The tarantula must **molt**. To molt means to shed the old skin. Tarantulas stop eating before they molt. Some tarantulas spin a silk pad to rest on during their molt.

To molt, the tarantula flips on its back or side. It moves itself back and forth until it is free of its old skin. A molt may last from two hours to two days. Tarantulas are weak during this time. Tarantulas' new skin is soft. It takes several days for it to become hard.

Tarantula bodies become whole when they molt. They can grow back missing legs, spinnerets, or fangs. Sometimes tarantulas flick off all the hairs from their abdomens. This leaves a bald spot. Those hairs grow back when the spider molts.

Young tarantulas molt from two to 10 times a year. Older, full-grown female tarantulas molt once a year or less. Males do not molt once they are adults.

This molting tarantula is pulling its legs out of its old skin.

Old Skin

The length of a tarantula's life depends on what kind it is. But all females live longer than males. Some female tarantulas can live 30 years or more. Males often die within a few days or a few months after they start mating. Some tree-living males may live up to two years after mating.

People must be careful when they handle their pet tarantulas.

Tarantulas and People

People and tarantulas have been living together for thousands of years. In the rain forest, tarantulas have been an important food for people. They wrap tarantulas in leaves, cook, and eat them.

Some people around the world keep tarantulas as pets. Tarantulas only need small spaces to live. People feed them mice, raw meat, or live insects, such as beetles or crickets.

Ground-living tarantulas can be easily hurt. Their abdomen could split if they are dropped. This could kill them. It is best to be careful when touching or picking up tarantulas.

▲ Tarantulas give warnings before they bite.
They raise their two front legs.

Tarantula Bites

Many people fear tarantulas. They believe that tarantulas will try to hunt and bite people. But this is not true. Tarantulas try to stay away from people. They often hide.

Tarantulas may bite if people scare them or try to pick them up. Some people say the bites feel like bee stings. The bites may become red and itch. But there are no known cases of people dying from tarantula bites.

Future of Tarantulas

People are cutting down the rain forest to build houses and clear land for farming. Many tarantulas lose their homes when this happens. Many kinds of tarantulas die when the rain forest is cut down. Some tarantulas can live near people. They may make their burrows on buildings, in old boxes, or holes in walls.

Some people think that selling tarantulas as pets may hurt the number of tarantulas in the wild. The Mexican redknee is one kind of common pet tarantula. So many are caught and sold that they are in danger of dying out in the wild.

The number of wild tarantulas is falling in many places around the world. People can keep them safe by working to save the forests where tarantulas live.

Glossary

abdomen (AB-duh-muhn)—the back part of a tarantula's body

adapt (uh-DAPT)—to change to fit well in a place

burrow (BUR-oh)—an underground hole or tunnel where an animal lives

cephalothorax (se-phuh-luh-THOR-aks)—the front part of a tarantula's body

chelicerae (ki-LI-suh-ray)—two body parts around spiders' mouths that are used like jaws

fang (FANG)—a long, pointed tooth

molt (MOHLT)—to shed the old outer skin in order to grow

nocturnal (nok-TUR-nuhl)—active at night

spiderling (SPYE-dur-ling)—a young spider

venom (VEN-uhm)—a poison made by some animals and insects that is pushed into their prey or enemies

Internet Sites

American Tarantula Society Page
http://atshq.org

Tarantula Planet
http://www.tarantulaplanet.org

Tarantulas@National Geographic.com
http://www.nationalgeographic.com/features/
97/tarantulas/introframe.html

Useful Addresses

American Arachnological Society
American Museum of Natural History
Central Park West at 79th Street
New York, NY 10024-5192

American Tarantula Society
P.O. Box 756
Carlsbad, NM 88221-0756

Index